MW01281750

CHILDREN
OF THE HOLLER

Growing up in Rush, Kentucky

JAMES A. ADKINS

Children of the Holler
Growing up in Rush, Kentucky
All Rights Reserved.
Copyright © 2020 James A. Adkins
v2.0

The opinions expressed in this manuscript are solely the opinions of the author and do not represent the opinions or thoughts of the publisher. The author has represented and warranted full ownership and/or legal right to publish all the materials in this book.

This book may not be reproduced, transmitted, or stored in whole or in part by any means, including graphic, electronic, or mechanical without the express written consent of the publisher except in the case of brief quotations embodied in critical articles and reviews.

Outskirts Press, Inc.
http://www.outskirtspress.com

ISBN: 978-1-9772-2132-2

Cover Photo © 2020 James Adkins. All rights reserved - used with permission.

Outskirts Press and the "OP" logo are trademarks belonging to Outskirts Press, Inc.

PRINTED IN THE UNITED STATES OF AMERICA

This is a story of growing up in Eastern Kentucky where poverty seemed to be all around, more so at our house.

Subtitle: This book could also be called Survival in The Holler, that is exactly what it was. Our family was very poor and dead broke most of the time we were in the head of the holler. Now for those who don't know head of the holler is the last house as far up the road as you can go. All the family did everything possible to make our lives as comfortable as possible, but here were many times I would think why try? The winters were always cold and snowy and the summer was equally hot and dusty or rainy and muddy. Living without running water and electricity was a struggle in its self, let alone the fact that most of the time descent food was at a minimum, had it not been for handouts from the county I don't know if we could have survived, especially in the winter months. But through it all we stuck together and Mom and Dad did all they could to raise us all with a decent education, taught us good manners and to be of good moral character, above all I guess we learned to respect all people and especially our elders. I know the upbringing we had created a special bond between all us kids at the time. Even today you can tell when we get together, you feel as though you are a member of some special OPS or something. I would like at this time to make mention of my three sisters, Sherry, Donna, and Myra and my younger brother Frank, who unfortunately, and very unexpectedly passed away in July of 2017. Frank was someone I could confide in and he was a great inspiration to not only me but the entire family. He was one that was always there to help anyone that needed help, was a very hard worker and just a great man. He truly is missed by all. My sisters were all in the same boat I was in. I know life in the holler was not always roses for them as well. They all shared in the chores and each one would do all they could to help. If that meant going on the hill to help get coal or wood in they were right there. Looking up at you with their rag-tag coat and hat on, worn out gloves and at least one untied shoe asking what I wanted them to do. So it is with much pride and forever gratitude that I would like to dedicate this book to my siblings. We all pulled the same sled. James A. Adkins

My father was a very hard working man, but the harder he tried, the behinder he got. Mom worked when she could, but she had a full time job trying to raise four children. Dad's good jobs were few and far between. When he did not have a regular job he would cut timber. Mostly pulp wood used for paper mills. I started working with him in the timber business when I was six. I carried a measuring stick and measured to the next cut. There wasn't much money to be made in the pulp wood business, thus my Mom had to find another way to feed us. She signed up for 'commodities' that the county gave away on the first of every month. That was some rough grub. I ate a lot of unleavened bread with cheese melted on it. Don't get me wrong, I was very thankful for our county food at the time.

I remember when we first moved to the head of the holler called Meadow Branch. That fall I was in the first grade. My Mom sent me off for my first day of school, which would turn out to be a nightmare for me.

It was a pretty morning, but wet and muddy. I had on a pair of white corduroy pants. I had to walk out of the holler alone to the bus stop. I was about ¼ mile to the first neighbor's house. As I approached their house I saw a huge black dog running from the neighbor's yard into the road. He was running straight for me, full speed; all I could see were his teeth. He lunged at me and bit me in the face knocking me into the ditch which was full of mud and water. By this time the dog owner finally saw what was going on and got the dog off of me. I was mud and blood from head to toe not to mention petrified with fear. I managed to get back to my house, no school that day. That is really about all I remember about that ordeal, but it was, at that time the scariest moment of my young life.

After the ordeal with the big black dog everything was back to normal. After a few days I was settled in school, I had my daily chores to do after school. We did not have electricity and we had to heat the house and cook with wood and coal. We could always go on one of our surrounding hills and gather wood. Coal, however was not quite so abundant, and we resorted to going to old coal and strip mines to try to find the coal. We would pick up what we could find and put it in an old feed sack and drag it off of the hill to the house. This would not be tolerated this day and time. As young children, my sisters and younger brother just accepted our life style and just went on as though all children lived like we did. In reality, all we had to do was go to school to see that was not so. Even though times were rough we still managed to deal with all the ups and downs.

Summer time wasn't nearly as bad as winter. We would pick black berries and sell them to people in the nearby little town. We would gather paw-paws and wild crab apples while we were out in the woods. In the fall of the year I remember laying in the sun on a log, eating, what we called opossum grapes. That was really just a wild grape but sweet and tasty. Occasionally my brother and I would catch bull frogs and fry them u over a camp fire in an old coffee can. Wouldn't want that now but they were great at the time. Sometimes we would sneak up on the hill to the old strip mine ponds and go swimming. I can remember swimming on one end of the pond and looking at the other end and see a snake swimming across the pond. After two or three years the neighbor with the big black dog moved away and what was to become my best childhood friend moved into their house.

Unlike children of today we had no means of communication. However, my friend and I learned how to whistle through our hands. If we wanted to get in touch we would whistle and the other would yell back to see what was up. Usually someone wanted you to go to the grocery store with them. Usually one would give his buddy 10 or 25 cents to go along. After all that was a walk over the hill and through the woods.

That old general store was where we could go for necessities, usually bread, sugar, coal-oil for lamps, whatever. I recall one trip with my oldest sister, we were sent to get one gallon of coal-oil (kerosene), 5 pounds of sugar and I don't know what else. The coal-oil was in a one gallon glass jug and the lid somehow leaked a little bit. My sister carried the sugar and I had the jug of oil. She started whining that the sugar was too heavy so I carried the coal-oil and the sugar in a bear hug.

When we got home we found out, much to my Mothers surprise the oil jug leaked and the bag of sugar absorbed it. Well, Mom did not throw it out, she made peanut butter fudge with it and it tasted just like kerosene. We were too poor to throw it away so we ate it and belched kerosene till the candy was all gone.

Even though we lived way back in the country you could not call our place a farm. It was old strip mine land and would not grow anything. My Father would on occasion bring something home that should have been on a farm. On one such occasion he brought home a pony. No saddle, just a pony and a bridle. I thought that was great! I was soon to reverse that thought. It was a hot summer day, kids alone at home and I decided to play cowboy with the new pony. I had watched the cowboys, on someone else's television, run and jump on their horse from behind. I thought I would try that. The pony was eating grass in our front yard and I caught him and put the bridle on, went well back behind him and ran to jump on and he started running. I ran after him and he stopped real quick and tried to kick me with both hind feet. The left hoof just missed the left side of my head but the right hoof caught me square in the nose. I thought I was dead. That pony almost ore my head off. I staggered to the front porch bleeding like a stuck hog. There were blood clots coming out of my nose the size of pencil erasers. I really thought I was going to die, funny thing was, I was the one at home in charge – seven or eight years old. Just walk it off! I looked like hell for two weeks.

I don't think I got in trouble over the pony ordeal, but I did get whipped a lot by Mom. I think she whipped me over stuff the other kids did. She would always whip me with whatever she could get her hands on first. I always said I was glad she wasn't coming by the chop block when she was going to whip me.

As I began to grow I soon realized I could out run my Mother. So, if she decided to whip me I would run and climb a tree. She would throw rocks at me! I would just climb higher, get out of her range and settle in. Then she would say, "just wait til your Daddy gets home'. Inside I would just chuckle because I knew Dad might not come home for two or three days. Later in the day when she would calm down I would come down from my tree.

If we were lucky enough to live through summer we had to get ready for fall and winter. Fall meant back to school, fall rains and knee deep mud. Our road out of the holler was just dirt and clay, no county gravel for us. I don't remember us having a car very often, when we did our road in and out was pretty much impassable in the fall and winter. We would walk about one half mile or so to catch the school bus, usually we carried our school shoes and wore our old shoes to walk in the pastures and hillside to our bus stop.

I really hated going to school, but naturally I had no choice. We didn't have money to pay for our lunch like most kids. We had to work for our lunch. A lot of times we would have to pick up trash outside around the school. I know some of the teachers looked at not only my family, but other less fortunate families as white trash. I will say this, after looking back at some of those teachers over the years it is very evident that

"Karma" has everyone's address. That's enough on that.

When the snows began in the late fall, usually mid November through late March, there would be patches of snow on the ground all winter. We did not have running water in our house, we would draw water in a bucket from an outside well. The bucket would set on a table by the cook stove in the kitchen. It would get so cold in our house at night that the water in the bucket would freeze.

There were fun times during the winter as well. Christmas was our favorite thing during the winter. At our church where we went to Sunday School was great at Christmas. After church on Christmas the deacons of the church stood at the door and gave out bags of treats to everyone as we left church. This usually consisted of an apple, an orange, a banana and some candy. We thought this was awesome! It really was at the time.

At home at Christmas we would always put up a Christmas tree and decorate it with strings of popcorn and homemade decorations. Mom and

Dad always done the best they could by us, but we all knew at Christmas, we kids had an ace in the hole – Mom-Maw Huff. She always made sure we all got at least one great gift! She truly was an angel on this earth! My other grandmother was good to us as well even though I have often been accused of being the favorite by one of my sisters, of course that was not so, she treated us all the same.

After Christmas and most of the time we made our toys and coal wagons out of whatever we could scrounge up. One of our most memorable toys was a used 20 inch bicycle given to us by my uncle Tim. It was the ultimate gift at the time. We also made our own fun stuff at times, at least I did. I remember teasing one of my sisters telling her that she was adopted. Mom would send me to the post office occasionally. On one trip I made up a fake letter for my sister and brought it to her saying I got it at the post office. It said in the letter that her natural parents were coming to get her. She believed it and cried until Mom came home from work.

We were always looking for something new to get into, as most children would. We played golf with walnuts and sticks with bends on the end. We made our own baseballs out of rags and tape and used big sticks as bats. We had lots of good times with our home made stuff.

There was an old cellar off to the side of our house in the backyard. The roof was gone but there were four stone walls and a doorway. In front of the cellar is where our well was located. All of our water came from this well. Behind the cellar was a giant Beech tree. I played a lot in this tree, and I would hide in it a lot when Mom was on the warpath. Behind the cellar and Beech tree was a great big rock that had a flat front on it, almost like a big wall. I would guess about eight feet high and 30 feet long. One day, when I wasn't busy, I used and old axe and carved my name in that rock, I guess I thought it would prove I was really there or something.

In the summer time my Mother always washed our clothes outside in a big metal tub. This meant carrying water from the well to fill the tub, and dragging firewood off the hill to build a fire around the tub to heat wash water. Needless to say, I hated wash day!

As I grew older, eight or nine, I found ways to get away from the holler, occasionally for a few days at a time. One way was to go to the store for Mom. I would ask the old man in the store if I could use his hone. He always said yes even though the phone was next door in his house. I would call my Paw-paw who lived in the city and ask him to come and get me, you know like it was his idea! He would always come to my rescue. This was my Moms Dad and she always let me go. I was in hog heaven for about a week, then back to the holler.

We had two country stores where we lived, they were two or three miles apart. There was an older couple in the community who decided to build a third store. They did, and it was a nice place, a lot of teen-age kids hung out there listening to the juke box and dancing. I was too young for that at the time and I was kind of overwhelmed by that crowd when I had to go there. You could hear the juke box a good half mile away. However the old lady who owned the store would always give us free candy and a lot of it. I guess she felt sorry for us.

I was at their store one day and the gentleman who owned it asked me if I would help him bleed the brakes on his truck. I was flattered and said I would even though I had no idea what he was talking about. Actually it was quite simple. All I had to do was pump the brake pedal for him. I know that doesn't sound like much, but that was one of my first mechanic jobs and I never have forgotten that. It wasn't too long a time after that the old gentleman passed away. It was like a death in the immediate family. They brought his body back home and set the casket u in the living room on display for visitation. That is how they did back then. I went to visit my old friend one last time. I had never seen a dead person before and I was scared to death. To this day every time I think of him, I'm glad I went.

As I look back I realize there were a lot of first time things in my life. Smoking comes to mind right off. I bought a pack of non-filter cigarettes, you know the manly kind. I went up around what was left of our old barn. I sat on the ground, built a little fire and lit my first smoke. I chain smoked seven or ten, all the time learning to inhale. Sick would be an understatement. I thought I was going to die. I threw the rest of the pack in the fire, I knew I wasn't ready for that!

Winter time was miserable in the holler. The road was virtually impossible to travel on . Coal and wood was needed then more than any time of the year. It got dark outside a lot earlier. Anyway, after chores and a little bite to eat, no matter the age, there was always homework. Abe Lincoln didn't have jack on me. I had to do my homework by a fireside light or kerosene lamp all winter long.

My Mother told me a story once when I was just a bay, someone, to this day I don't know who, but someone offered to trade my Mom and Dad a brand new car for me! I have often wondered what it? In reality I'm glad they didn't trade.

As I stated earlier, my Father was a hard worker. He had several different jobs. One job he had was servicing and replacing has station pumps. The guy he worked wit was a religious sort, he would not eat meat on Friday. Hey, no problem, I am good with that, I'm just telling a story. However, Dad would come home every Friday evening about half lit and he always had a box of frozen fish sticks! We knew what we were having for super every Friday as long as he kept that job. He also drove a Volks Wagon van while on this job. The van had huge storage pockets on the inside of the front doors. This is where Dad kept his Vodka hid. My little brother and I knew this so one Friday evening we slipped out to the old bug van and got us a little drink. It was like drinking fire, nothing but snot and tears! Dad told me later the reason he drank Vodka was because Mom couldn't smell it on him. He couldn't walk but no one could smell it.

Since I'm on the subject of seafood I remember one of my neighbors and I caught three or four big snapping turtles. We asked Mom if she would fry them up if we cleaned them and she said she would so we did our part. Beautiful white meat and it did taste like chicken!

Outside of selling blackberries for a month or so, there weren't very many money making opportunities for kids back then. We could sell pop bottles for three cents a piece that we picked up along the main road at the mouth of the holler, but one old man down at the end of our road loved to fish. He said he would pay a penny a piece for grasshoppers. You talk about a circus! You should have seen three or four kids in the middle of a cow pasture chasing grasshoppers that could jump and fly ten to twenty feet at a time. Not a very lucrative business.

Around our place we had certain land marks we would refer to so all the kids knew where we were talking about when these landmarks were given as a reference point. There are three that come to mind, Bear Mountain, Blue Pond and Pikes Peak. Bear Mountain was the last big hill in the very head of the holler where we lived. Blue Pond was an old strip mine pond up a little holler behind our house. It was real dark water, and eerie looking. We actually stayed away from it. Pikes Peak was a big tall hill and it only had two identical oak trees standing on top. You could see this hill from the main highway when leaving our community.

One time I land a job on the other side of Bear Mountain. I must have been over in there just out exploring. Anyway, a man who lived over there offered me fifty cents an hour to cut brush off a hill behind his house and he furnished the tools. Naturally I said I would do it. I hurried home that day and told Mom all about it and she was ok with me doing it. I don't remember how long I worked there but it was a good job for me at the time. I remember mom fixing me a lunch and sending it to me by my brother and sister. We did not have a coffee bottle so Mom put coffee in a quart jar and wrapped it in a towel so it would be warm when I got it. Where I was working was about an eighth of a mile from the main road. I was on a hill behind a house actually out of sight. I could see the main road real good. There was a slight grade and a curve in the road. When I would take a break, I would sit down and watch and listen to the big rigs all downshift in the same spot. Not knowing at the time how contagious the big rigs were to my inner soul.

This also reminds me of the time that my Dad had a truck driving job. I walked out of the holler one morning on my way to catch the school bus.

There it sat, parked beside the road at the end of our road. It was a bright yellow diesel truck! It looked as big as a two story house to me. You could smell diesel fuel and rubber when I got close to it and the wind deflector (bug knocker) on the hood said "Baby Doll". I will never forget that. I think that is where my passion for big trucks actually started.

I did learn how to drive on my neighbors hay truck. I told him I would help him get hay in for fifty cents a day, not hour but day, if he would let me drive and he agreed. I didn't care about the money, I just wanted to learn to drive. I think I was about 12 or 13 years old at the time.

Above our house by our old barn was a very steep grade that was the remnants off an old coal storage pile. It was mostly fine coal and dirt. We called it the slack pile. If you could come up with a big piece of cardboard, it made the perfect slicky slide, although a very dirty one.

Another form of entertainment was swinging on grapevines. Swinging out over big rocks and hillsides was a blast. I was swinging one day, alone, having a big time. I got a big run and swung out over the hillside. At about the top of my flight the grapevine broke! It seemed like I fell forever! I landed on my back with my head pointed downhill. I could not breathe, I thought I was dying. It was the first time I had ever had the breath knocked out of me. Anyway, I got my breath back, got up and shook it off and went off in search of another swing. We usually had two or three spots with grapevine swings but the one that broke with me was everyone's favorite.

The main road at the mouth of our holler had always been just an old gravel road. Someway, somehow, it was now being blacktopped. We could not believe it! A race track! The job was completed in mid-summer. My buddy and I thought it would be a good idea to play a Halloween trick in mid-July and catch everyone on new road off guard. We decided to block the road. We found a spot with a blind spot in the road. There was a rise in the road and no one could see over it very well. We went on the hill and pulled brush into the road, nothing big because we were too little to get big stuff. We also had to be as quiet as we could because you could not hear the cars approaching on the newly surfaced road like you could on the gravel. We finished piling the brush on the road and ran up on the hill to hide and wait. It wasn't long until we heard a car coming. Loud and fast. They got to the blind spot and popped over the rise, brakes locked and tires squalling. They didn't even stop and brush went everywhere. We waited around for another car or two but one stopped and said to his friend that we were probably hiding on the hill watching. He said he ought to shoot up in the brush where we were. Anyway, he left and we decided we had had enough Halloween in July so we cleaned up the road and got out of there. Back over the hill to the holler and home. We never did do that again.

I know I said we did not have electric in our old house, but I found out later it was actually wired and somehow the electric was on for a little while. I remember us getting a television somewhere, and the first TV show I really remember watching was Bonanza. However shortly after that our wiring caught on fire, no real damage but that was the end of our electricity in that house.

Somehow I managed to come by an old 12 gauge shotgun, I had a good beagle dog that my grandfather had given me. He was the real deal, registered and everything. His only problem was he was way too fat. His name was Rex and he had a beautiful deep bark when he was after a rabbit. Only problem was if the rabbit he was after started up hill, the race was over. One beautiful fall day, Rex and I were hunting back on the ridge that bordered one of the neighbors. I happened to look up in a giant oak tree which just happened to be on the property line and there high in the top was a bunch of Mistletoe in it. Christmas wasn't that far off so I thought if I could get it down I could sell it. There were no limbs on this tree, except near the top, so I could not climb it. I didn't want to shoot it out for fear of damaging it so I decided to cut it down. Big mistake! A day or two later I slipped back on the hill and I starting chopping. Halfway into the day the big tree fell. I gathered my mistletoe and headed home. I was real proud of my bounty and I took it in to show my Mom. That went pretty good, but not good. She wanted to know where I got it, so I told her and I told her the truth. It had barbwire on it and was on the property line. Well, she went wild. She made me go to the neighbors house and tell him what I had done. So I did. I was scared and embarrassed to tell him but he was very understanding and nice about it. No problem, I think he liked me, unknowing to Mom I would go down and hang out with this old gentleman at his barn every once in a while. He was a Grandfather figure to me.

I was getting into late fall, we were back in school. The days were getting cooler and much shorter. We had a little bus house at the mouth of the holler where we would catch the school bus. There was a time or two that I would climb up in the loft of the bus house and hide until the bus ran. I would then go back home and tell Mom I missed the bus. I didn't lie! I did miss it! I noticed one morning while boarding the school bus that the valve on the wheel had a built in valve core remover on it. Yeah, I guess a little bulb went on over my head. The bus driver lived about three and a half miles from where I caught the bus. The railroad track at my bus stop ran right by where he parked the bus. The bus was parked between the railroad and his house. One night I walked all the way to the bus, staying on the railroad. When

I got there it was dark, I'm thinking this was a t Halloween and we were out trick or treating. Anyway, I slipped down by the front of the bus and took the valve cap off and barely loosened the valve core. Just enough to where you could hear the air coming out. The next morning we were getting ready for school, we all gathered at the bus stop and waited and waited and waited. No bus, no school. I grinned all the way back home. If mom had known what her little boy had done.

Well, as I stated before winter was fast approaching. That meant getting in all the coal we could find at the old strip mines. We would try to make the best of it while on the hill. There were a few shallow ponds and they were frozen over most of the winter. This is where we would get a couple of long sticks and a piece of coal and play ice hockey. Like I said before, in those days we had to make our fun.

Sometimes in the fall or early winter, we were lucky enough to get one or two pairs of five buckle arctic boots to wear over our shoes in the mud and snow. Of course all the children shared them. Just depended on who was going on the hill or to the store. The quickest way to ruin these boots was to tear a hole in one. Which was very easily done. A sharp rock, snag or hidden piece of barbed wire is usually what made a tear in our boots. However, when that happened, we had a rubber boot patch kit. Monkey Grip was the name of the boot patch. It worked great, and I will always remember that product name.

One winter day I was coming home from the store and stopped by a friend's house, down on the main road. Just so happened they had a bunch of puppies they were giving away. Cute little fuzzy shepherd of some kind. I picked out a little boy, put him in a cardboard box and brought him home. Then I asked mom if we could keep him. Since we did not have a dog at the time, she said we could keep him. My little brother wanted to name him Ringo. You can guess where he came up with that name! Anyway, we loved our new pup. This gave us something to do with that nasty powdered milk we got in the commodities every month. We used it as formula for Ringo. Ringo grew up to be a beautiful brown and white shepherd dog. He was a great watch dog. Not much of a hunter, but he was the best snake dog in the county. He hated all snakes and there is no way we could count how many he killed over the years. We kept him for years and when we finally moved out of state we took him with us, he was family.

While we were living in the last house in the holler, there were four of us kids. However, my Mother became pregnant with my youngest sister while we lived there. One cold November night, the time came to go to the hospital. Mom had to walk out of the holler to the car. All went well, she had to stay in the hospital for a couple of days. All us kids stayed home and cleaned house and had it good and warm for Mom and our new sister when they came home. We were even good! The only downfall to this was that my rabbit dog, Rex, followed Mom out of the holler on her way to the hospital and got hit by a train. That was a bad deal, all I could do was cry and let it go.

The following summer the house below us became vacant. Much to the delight of all of us kids, Mom and Dad rented it! We all chipped in and helped Mom clean the new place and we carried all of our belongings and furniture to the new house. I think it took us about a week to move. The new place did not have running water, but it did have electricity! It was still tough going for the next few years, we still had days of "water gravy". If you know what I mean. I'm sure some know that its flour and water without milk for gravy. With this move we didn't have to walk quite as far to catch the school bus, although it was still a long wet muddy walk most of the time. Now I was older and a little bigger as far as being able to work a big boy job. I still helped Dad in the timber cutting business when school was out for the summer. Dad had a life long friend that was his partner in the timber work. We did not have any high tech tools to work with. We had a couple of chain saws and a team of mules to drag the logs out of the woods. I was the one who followed the mules all day. One day I remember very well, I was trailing the mules down a long haul road with four logs. Everything was going good, the mules were making a very easy downhill pull, hardly any strain on them at all. Just going at a good steady pace the jingle of the harness kind of in rhythm to the sound of their hooves on the hard ground. Suddenly the mules just froze in place, dead stopped. It was dead quiet and then I heard a buzzing g sound. It sounded like a jar fly, a giant fly with huge wings. It made the buzzing noise again and then I saw it, on the left side of the haul road, in the weeds. All coiled up was a giant diamond back rattlesnake that was probably the worst scare of my life! I turned and ran back up the hill and started yelling for Dad. He was in the process of cutting a tree down but he heard me yelling above the noise of the chainsaw! He shut the saw off and I told him what was going on. Well he came running and I was hoping he would kill the snake. Instead, much to my surprise, he cut a forked stick and put the fork behind the sakes head then took a piece of rawhide string off of the mules harness and tied one end behind the snakes head and one end to the stick and picked it up! He then put it in a big jar of some kind and punched holes in the lid and gave it to one of the onlookers who had gathered by now. There was one condition, the guy had to take it by our house and show it to my Mom! I thought that was mean because Mom hated snakes as much as I did.

The timber that my Dad and his partner were cutting just happened to belong to the local bootlegger. On some days when we had a lunch break some of the good ole boys would come around and before you knew it there was a poker game going and they would get to drinking. Dad and his buddy could get their whiskey and put it on their timber account. I would just find a comfortable spot out of the way. I figured all work was pretty well done for the day. I remember one day Jake, Dads partner, really drank his fill and by the end of the day he had passed out cold. Jake owned the mules I used to drag logs with so I had to take Jake and the mules home. We threw Jake over one of the mules, looked like a dead outlaw in an old western movie! I rode the other mule and led the mule hauling Jake up the main road for all to see. We rode about two miles to Jakes house and then to the barn. I put the mules inside and drug Jake off the back of his mule. I was just a skinny little boy and Jake was about 175 pounds so he hit the ground pretty hard. He didn't even open an eye! Real good whiskey I guess. I removed the harness from the team and hung it on the wall, put the mules in their stalls and fed and watered them. I walked about 100 yards to Jakes house and told his mother he was laying over in the entrance way of the barn, drunk. She seemed to take it all in stride, all of her sons drank like that.

When I was very young, about eight to eleven years old I would stay with my Grandmother Adkins quite a bit. She would always take care of me no matter the situation. At one time there was a bad case of Measles going around, they were called German measles and I came down with them. Just so happened I was at my Mom-maws house at the time. I was sick for two weeks. I mean bad sick! That stuff was deadly and I was medicated with all kinds of stuff but the one I remember most as sassafras tea. This was made from the tender twig bark from a Sassafras tree, boiled to perfection by my Grandmother. I guess it helped, I got better but the best medicine I received besides the love and attention was all the ice cream I got to eat. You know, it helped keep my temperature down. While staying with my Grandmother I got to watch a lot of TV. One of my favorite shows was the old western "Tales of Wells Fargo". I loved Jim Hardy. For Christmas one year Mom-maw bought me one of my most cherished gifts ever. It was a toy horse with the rider, hat, saddle, rifle and pistol – none other than Jim Hardy and his horse! I remember playing with that for hours at a time. I still have it today, sitting majestically on a shelf in my library. Priceless!

I spent a lot of my childhood with my Grandmother and my Uncles and cousins on the Adkins farm, but now all I have is the memories. They have all passed on and the land and old house were sold off. The new owner tore down the house and all that was there. He then landscaped with a dozer and he did a great job. Now when you see the old farm, you cannot tell there ever was a house or anything there. It is still a beautiful piece of property with many memories.

I often refer to my childhood, along with my brother and sisters, as the depression of the fifties. That's what it was like at the time. I'm sure a lot of our friends and neighbors never had all they wanted back then, but everyone seemed to come up with what they needed.

Thankfully all us kids seemed to be pretty healthy. Maybe a little skinny, but healthy. My little brother had a time every winter with whooping cough, this was when he was very young. I would guess when he was five to eight years old. Seemed like every time he would go to town or somewhere with Dad, Dad would come back without him. Brother would get sick and be in the hospital.

Winter was rough on us all back then. When the snows came it made it very hard to find dry wood, and really rough trying to go to the old strip mines and find coal but I don't ever remember coming off the hill empty handed! That was not an option when your heating and cooking depended on what you brought in. I can remember cold winter nights when it would snow and the wind would blow so hard you could see snow come in around our front door and the windows. One year my Mother put plastic over the windows outside to keep the cold out. At that time we had a big goat that just ran free outside and one night the goat ate the plastic covering around the outside living room window! I guess he must have been really hungry. My Mother was furious! I can't remember whatever happened to that goat. It seemed as though the winter was 12 months long, but finally the sun would be out longer and hotter and patches of dirt and dead grass could be seen as winters white blanket began to leave the holler.

Springtime was definitely a welcome time of the year for us kids. We no longer had to deep a fire going all night and we could play outside without getting too cold. Muddy, but not cold. Springtime meant that summer was just around the corner and school would be out for summer vacation in just a few weeks. Even though it did get extremely hot in the holler in July and August, summer was still our favorite time of year. We were out of the house from early morning until dark every day. I'm sure Mom liked that even though I know she worried about us when we were all running the hills and swimming in the old strip mind ponds.

One of my most enjoyable past times when I was a young boy was playing basketball out in front of our house. The ball was usually whatever I could come up with. The rim was an old bicycle wheel with the spokes removed and nailed to a Walnut tree out by the coal pile. I did finally come up with a real basketball and a real basketball rim no net. Anyway I spent countless hours shooting baskets and playing imaginary games in the coal dust out by that old Walnut tree.

One of our neighbors brought in fish from a pay lake that he went to quite often and put them n one of the old strip mine ponds. So I decided after a while to go there and fish. Trouble was, I did not have any fishing gear so I made some. A pole was easy, I found some of Moms thread for my line but I did not have a hook. I finally decided to use a stick pin. I bent it into the shape of a hook and tied my ine just under the cap of the pin, found me some worms under an old board and off I went to the strip pond. The hook actually worked, even though it did not have a barb on it. I found that if you just held a slight pressure on the line you could land you a fish! I caught two or three that day even though they were small. It was catch and release for me anyway. I was just glad that my homemade fishing gear worked!

Even though we could not buy stuff to play with, we always made everything. To me that was half the fun of it, especially if our new inventions worked as planned.

Our old house did not require very much up keep by us kids, never did any painting or white washing on the old house even though we did pain the old tin roof one time that I remember. Dad came up with a five gallon bucket of red paint from somewhere. The old house was actually pretty solid for its age. I would guess it was built in the thirties. It was a seven room log structure with wood siding, three big porches around the house and of course the tin roof. Four of the rooms had a fireplace, old grates and most of the heat went up the chimney but luckily, no one froze to death. My Mother kept the place as clean as possible, which I'm sure was a job with four kids tracking in mud and snow all the time. I remember when it would rain hard in the summer, sitting on the front porch on an old couch and taking in the sound and smell of the pouring rain. It was quite relaxing. I really liked the sound of the rain hitting the old tin roof at night. Even though I knew the rain always turned our old road and yard into a mud bog, the air always smelled so fresh and clean after those summer rain storms. Living like we did, and where we did taught me a lot of life's lessons, big and little, good and bad, and I abide by them to this day and very thankful for every one of them. Sometimes life itself is the greatest teacher of all. Being raised in the holler, being brought up rough, doing without a lot of things has no doubt made a lifelong effect on me, my sisters and my brother without a doubt, but over the years as I look back I can honestly say my childhood was and still is a very positive experience for me, and I am sure my siblings would all agree.

One thing I can recall us having to replace was a bridge just below our house. The old one was made of wood and it just rotted away and was not safe to run a vehicle over. This was a big deal for us kids. My Dad and some of his friends actually roe the old bridge out and put in new logs for the base and then put new boards on it. It was still good when we moved out of the holler. We were always carrying rocks, big and small, to fill up ruts and big mud holes so the road would be somewhat passable. In the winter time you mostly had to walk in and out of the holler even if we were lucky enough for the family to have an old car. Back then if your politics were right the county would bring a load of red dog gravel and put it on your road. I guess mom and Dad were not registered to vote! Every once in a while in the summer the county would send a road grader to the holler. They would smooth out the ruts and holes. Ina few days we would get a big rain and the road would be good and muddy again and some of Dads friends would run a big dual wheel truck in and out of the holler tearing our road all to hell. Just more mud and ruts all over again!

There was not very many ways a young boy could make a little spending money in the holler. Our resources, natural or otherwise were extremely limited. One day I got the bright idea of cutting timber, a load of pulp wood. I asked one of my cousins if he wanted to help and I offered him a 50/50 split. He was all for it. Now at this time I was about 13 years old, my cousin was a couple of years older than me. Now mind you, we had no timber tools, just a big idea! Somehow we came up with a cross-cut saw. For those of you who don't know, this saw is powered by man-power, one on each end, push, pull , pure muscle.

The trees we were going to cut were pine. They had to be cut in five foot lengths and had to be close to the road because we did not have any way to drag logs out of the woods. Now sawing up pine on a hot summer day with a cross-cut is hard work. Even for a big man, let alone two 120 pound boys. The resin, or sap, in a pine tree would really make it hard to push and pull the saw so we kept a jug of kerosene with us to pour on the saw blade when it started to bind up. We finally cut enough pulp wood to make a load, even though it was a small one. Next, we had to find someone with a flatbed truck to haul our wood to market. We had to load the truck by hand, me and my cousin, and when we got it to the buyer, we had to unload it onto a rail-car. I think the load brought somewhere around twenty two dollars. After we paid the haul bill, I think we each made about six or seven dollars. I think I could have made more money than that searching for and selling pop bottles. I did work in timber more, in upcoming years, but never again with a cross-cut saw.

I would stay with my Mom-maw Adkins as much as I could when school was out for the summer.

I would help in the fields as much as I could. I can remember following my Uncle Carl around while he used a horse and plow to plow the fields. He would plow all day, stopping only to eat dinner around noon and then work until five or six in the evening, take care of the old plow horse for the day then wash up for supper. A lifestyle kind of like an old TV western. When the corn started to grow I would sometimes help by getting a hoe and digging out a few weeds. I know it was awful hot and I thought I was helping. Didn't take me long to figure out farming was a lot of hard work.

Every year in the fall when it was cold outside my Dad and my uncles would have a hog killing. It may sound a little morbid but I loved watching their routine from start to finish. That day you would get pork tenderloin as fresh as possible. Straight from the hog to the skillet. My Grandmother was without a doubt one of the best cooks in all of Kentucky and that is a lot of good cooks. To this day I have never found one any better. I guess one reason she was so good was she had a lot of practice. She had 13 children.

*Entry to the home site. Water and mud
after the summer drought in 2019*

Home site. House is no longer
standing, just an empty wet field

*Top of the Beech tree where I ran to
safety from Mom when she was mad*

The 'J' I carved in my rock

The roofless cellar

*The church I attended. They still hold
regular services to this day*

Mawmaw Adkins home place. The house and barn are no longer standing, it's an empty field

*The one room school house I
attended located in Music, KY*

The store I used to go to

Aerial view of my home site showing landmarks

Mom-maws farm consisted of 400 acres. It had two small ponds with fish, lot sof bottom land with a creek and lots and lots of hills and woods. This was an awesome place for a young boy to romp, play and explore. It did not matter what the season I always had a lot of fun there. Memories, one sad thing I witnessed on the farm happened up around the barn one day. My uncle was digging a hole out by the barn. He was using a post hole digger. Come to find out he was digging a grave for a baby pig. I did not know what the deal was with this little pig, but I do remember crying when I saw my uncle put the pig in the hole. I was probably seven or eight years old and at that time I had not witnessed very much death of any sort. Most of the time everything at Mom-maws was pretty good. I guess she did pamper me a little bit. Her house was always warm and cozy in the fall and winter. There was plenty of good food and pop and candy, if you knew where to look. The good stuff was never too hard to find. Summertime there was amazing as well. I think what really stands out in my mind about Mom-maws place was the sights, sounds and smells of the holiday season. Thanksgiving and Christmas. All my Aunts and Uncles would come home at holiday time. You talk about a feed! Those gals could cook. Thanksgiving and Christmas dinners were the greatest. It seemed like there were enough leftovers at Thanksgiving to eat on for two weeks. Christmas dinner was about the same way. Undoubtedly some of the best times of my childhood.

On these holiday get togethers my Dad and my uncles would always go out rabbit hunting while the women were preparing the big meal. They would let me go with them. I always had a lot of fun when I went along. Dogs running, and shotguns blasting. It really was a good time for a young boy back then. After the hunt we would all gather back at Mom-maws. The house was always warm and cozy and the smell of all the holiday food was as good as it gets.

After the big meal the men would all settle in the living room around the big pot belly stove and smoke and talk while the women were cleaning up in the kitchen. You could hear occasional laughter from the women and I knew they were having a good time as well. After everything was cleaned up and the kitchen was back to normal the women would come to the living room and after a brief visit everyone would start to leave. I figured I would see some of them every once in a while at Mom-maws but I knew we all would not be together again until the next big holiday. It was always a great time and I do miss those days.

Powdered milk and powdered eggs. I ate so much rice back then I'm surprised that I did not have slanted eyes. Oh yeah, we also had the famous government cheese that every one rants and raves about. I would like to hear what they would say about it if you had to eat it on an unleavened pancake three times a day. Don't get me wrong, I am very glad we had the commodities, I don't know what our family would have done without them.

Before moving to the head of the holler we lived in an old house about three or four miles on up the main road, actually, it was at the end of the main road, a little country community called Music. There was a one room school there. I was just starting the first grade. This school had one teacher, grades first through eighth. Of course there was no air conditioning and the school was heated in the winter with a big pot belly stove. Using coal for fuel, The temperature varied depending on which boys put coal in the stove, sometimes it would get cherry red. This school looked like you were living in the old west. You know, like on the prairie or something like that. I know one thing for sure, the teacher sure earned her money on that job. I did not go to Music school very long before we moved up in the holler. I'm glad I got a little taste of the one room school experience though.

One of the worst things about the holler, of course winter time, trying to get in and out. The snows sometime seemed to make time stand still because you were stranded. One time right around Christmas my Grandparents were bringing Christmas gifts to us and the road was so bad they could not get all the way to our house. There was an old hollow tree beside the road, that was a monster tree in size. My Mom-maw put our Christmas gifts inside that old hollow tree and I guess they told one of our neighbors at the mouth of the holler what they had done and when the neighbor saw some of our family they passed on the message. Santa Claus made it again. I guess we had all been good little boys and girls. Not! One of the best Christmas gifts I can remember getting was a 9volt transistor radio. My Maw-maw Huff got it for me when I was nine or ten years old. I would listen to it late at night under the covers in the old dark house. It opened up a whole new world that I hoped to be able to see some day. I would listen to my radio until the battery would run down and then I would take the battery out of the radio and set it just on the edge of Moms cook stove and let it warm up. This would recharge the battery for a little while. Then I would repeat.

During the 1950's our country was in good economic condition. Everywhere except in Kentucky especially the eastern part of the state. The coal market was way off in the late fifties and a lot of miners were out of work. Most of them had been miners all of their working life and really had no other means of making a living. When the mines slowed up so did all the coal related jobs. The whole economy in eastern Kentucky was greatly affected. Just so happened we were being brought up in a very depressed area at this time in our lives. One of the other natural resources during this time was timber and it was depleting at a very high rate. If it had not been for timber and commodities I really don't think we could have made it in the head of the holler as long as we did. The ground around our house was pretty much waste land, lots of mud and rock run off from the old strip mines over the years. The ground was more like shale rock than regular soil. You could not grow anything there and the yard that was in front of our house was awful, it was about one third swamp and it stayed wet and muddy the year around caused by runoff from an old strip mine pond about 300 years or so on the hill behind our house. I am not whining about my childhood, I am just saying times were hard and things were bad back then, all around, it just seemed to be very bad in the head of that cold, muddy holler.

By now one of my greatest desires was wanting to learn to drive. I knew I could do it, I just needed a chance to drive. Finally, I was old enough to take drivers education in school. That all went great. I was the first in our class to take the driver's test. I persuaded my Driving Teacher to let me take the driving test. He said I wasn't ready but he agreed. I made a 98% on my test, it should have been 100% but the cop giving the test screwed up! Honest! Now I was on cloud nine but I did not have a car. I knew I was going to have to find me a job after school hours. Mom and Dad did well to keep a family car, I knew they couldnt get me one, nor did I expect them to. That's just not how things went in those days.

As luck would have it, I did find a job! A new service station went in about five miles from our house, right beside the interstate. This was a full service gas station. I got a job working evenings and weekends. My job was to pump gas, change oil, grease jobs, fix tires, wash cars, everything involved in service station work in those days. It was great, I was making a little money and I enjoyed it. I was and always have been a car guy, I just didn't know it then. Anyway, we had a regular customer who drove an ambulance, a real nice middle aged gentleman who lived up my way. One day he stopped in driving a 55 Ford 4 door. It was for sale! I asked him how much he wanted for the car. He ghought for a little bit and said $125.00. I asked him if I could make payments on it, leave it at his house until it was paid for and he agreed! I think he liked me, one reason I always worked on his cars for him and dropped them off at his house. I could hardly wait to get home and tell Mom about the deal I had made. She was actually OK with it, but insisted that she and I go down to the man's house and talk about the details, I guess so she knew all the details which was fine with me. I paid some on that car every week, and it was soon paid for. It was just an old 4 door Ford, but at that time it was the greatest car around to me. That old Ford, turned out, was just one of many that I owned while in the holler. There were lots of mechanical failures and a few wrecks along, the first years of driving.

As far as working while in school, I was very fortunate to have a job most of the time. After I quit working at the service station I went to work at a truck stop about a mile or so on down the road. The truck stop was easier to work around my school schedule.

One of the few pleasures for me in walking in and out of the holler when I was a young lad was seeing the horses on the neighbors farm. One in particular was a young thorough bred by the name of Molly. She was a beautiful young mare. She was always running and prancing around in the pasture field and another pretty horse was actually a young Shetland pony on our Landlords farm. His name was Prince and that's what he was to me. Both of these horses were beautiful, majestic animals and looked so out of place, alone in the holler.

Somewhere I came up with another shotgun. A 12 gauge automatic. It must have been another gift from my Grandfather. Anyway, it was a lot of fun to hunt with. One of my good friends told me about a place on their farm that was loaded with squirrels, but they did not want anyone to hunt there. Well sure enough, one day I slipped through the barbed wire fence, crossed the creek and headed up the ridge to the forbidden ground. It was like being in a big park! No underbrush and filled with giant Oak and Beech trees. This was squirrel heaven. The trees were alive with squirrels, red and gray! It was like a giant shooting gallery. I don't remember how many I got that day, but I know it sounded like a young war! Adrenaline was maxed out! I was about half a mile from the land owners house so I gathered up my furry bounty and hurried home.

As I got a little older I started to realize it was getting harder and harder to make something out of nothing so I started looking for a real after school, in the evening, job. One of those jobs I happened to come by was waxing a mobile home for one of my neighbors. Fifty cents a foot! I thought I had hit the big time. I instantly started figuring length and width and figuring up the dollars. I got out a ladder, wax and rags and went to work. By the time I finished that trailer seemed like it was a mile long and half a mile wide. My right arm felt like it was about to fall off. To this day I can't remember if I completed that job or not.

I also worked for this family in the hay fields. Back then everything was square bales, you would usually pick them up behind the hay baler and load them onto a trailer or flat bed truck. The old swimming hole sure looked good after working in the hay fields all day.

Some people around where we lived would make a little extra money by selling scrap iron and metal. Usually in the form of an old junk car. But you really need a good sized truck if you were going to junk. Since I had neither a truck or any junk I did not get into that business.

My Sister and I both worked in grade school for our lunch, prior to that there were time when we would take our lunch to school. Usually a hard biscuit with cheese or peanut butter on it. We really were fortunate to get to work a little for our hot lunch. The majority of the grade school kids we went to school with had no idea what real work was like.

We moved to the next house, the one with electric, about the time I started high school. Everything seemed to be getting better for our family then. Dad was working a steady decent job. I was working at school and after school. We also had a new baby sister now, luckily for her she did not have to go through all the hardships of living in the head of the holler. Don't get me wrong, we were still poor as church mice, but times were better. Heck, we could even take our old truck and go buy a load of coal once in a while!

Now going to high school was a whole different world for me. Unlike our grade school out in the country, the high school was in the city. We still rode the school bus, but it was still culture shock for this ole head of the holler boy! It was pretty easy to tell the haves from the have not's. A lot of the kids, much to my surprise were just as poor as our family, but I don't think they had quire the rugged childhood as me, my brother and sisters did. That was a good thing!

You could easily tell the kids who came from well to do families. They naturally had the best shoes and clothes money could buy, and mommy would drop them off at school in her new car. I did see a few hard cases as far as being poor was concerned, but I do not recall anyone making fun or teasing someone about not having fancy shoes or clothes. It was almost as if the well to do realized how lucky they were not to be poor. Thus they did not ridicule anyone. They probably did not want a good country butt-whuppin either.

Our second house in the holler was five rooms and a path. All the older country people will know what the path refers to. Still no running water, but the well had a well box and a rope and pulley for drawing water. That made getting water in a lot easier. The place also had a decent outbuilding and shed out back. The shed was a great place for cutting wood and storing coal.

Everyday life was just easier after we moved out of the head of the holler. The families over all economic state were better. I don't mean that we had money to waste by any stretch of imagination but we were able to quit getting commodities from the county. I for one was very thankful for that. Nothing like real food after you had been eating that county food for all those years.

As the high school years moved along I continued to work at the gas station and truck stop. I really liked the old truck stop job. My senior year of high school I took just enough classes to gradu-ate. This way I got out of school at noon. I would then go home and sleep during the evening, go to work at the truck stop, get off around seven in the morning, take a shower and get breakfast, then go onto school. If I had an old car I would drive. If not, I would catch a ride with one of the big rigs. I always liked riding in the big rigs, the main highway ran right in front o four school and I always thought it was cool to get out of a tractor trailer at the red light in front of our school.

By now I had pretty well got the best of my old 56 Ford and so I had traded around and had three or four other old cars by my senior year in high school. I do remember as a senior in high school all the other guys in school had the cool hot rods, some even had new Mustangs and Camaros. Those were the "Haves". Me, I was driving a 1952 Chevy truck, six cylinders, three speed on the column. I love it! I wish I had that old truck today. I used it for hauling wood and coal or just whatever needed to haul. One year after Christmas we took our old Christmas tree down and I threw the old tree in the back of the truck. I hauled it around until March before finally throwing it out somewhere.

Before too much longer it would be time to graduate high school. I was so looking forward to that, because I actually hated school, I thought this must be what jail is like. Deep down I knew better, but I still hated it. I made pretty good grades for someone who hardly ever took a book home. I could have done so much better if I had only tried. I guess I wanted to get out of the holler, out in the real world.

One rainy spring day, Mom wanted to go to town so we could get some new clothes for me to wear to graduation. We were about two or three miles from home, I was driving Dads truck. We were coming into an S curve at a railroad crossing. I saw a car coming toward us going way too fast for the wet road, as he approached the S curve I saw his front wheels lock up. At that point he had no control. I ran through a ditch line and went completely off the road trying to avoid the car. No use, he hit Dads truck, hard on the driver's side. Thankfully no one was hurt, but it totaled the truck. Only good thing was I had mom with me as my witness that it wasn't my fault, so I didn't have to face the wrath of dear old Dad. I loved that old truck, it was a V-8 Ford 3 speed transmission, and was a fast truck. Not saying I ever raced it, but it never lost!

Anyway, after the accident with Dads truck, we managed to get ready for graduation. On May 28th 1968 I did just that! So thankful that my Mother made me get up every morning to school and made me go when I wanted to quit. At the time I graduated, it was common for high school seniors to go on a senior trip. Our school usually went to Washington, D.C. but not the year I graduated. According to the higher ups, there was too much civil unrest in our country for a trip. I guess, I probably would not have gone anyway.

At that time most healthy boys who did not go to college, get married, or whose family was politically connected knew where their senior trip was going to be. Viet Nam. No one talked about it much, but it was always in the back of your mind. You had a high school diploma in one hand, and a !A draft card in the other. Wasn't too hard to figure. Back then, I'm proud to say, I don't know of anyone who resisted going in the service. Not that anyone was crazy about the idea, but it was a patriotic duty, and was viewed upon just that way. Yeah, I know of a few Rambo's who enlisted as soon as school was out. For the most part everyone just went to work and waited for their number to be called and some hoped that political war would end before they had to go. They still remained ready.

During this time, Dad had a good job, working out of state, doing construction work, but he was home every day. I was still working at the truck stop and doing odd jobs all the while now that I was out of school, I was looking for a real job. One of my odd jobs was working in timber, again, but it was only on Saturday. A couple of my older friends had real jobs, but played around in the timber business more as a hobby I think because they both had good jobs. They paid me eight dollars to drag logs for them, on this one day a week deal. That was good at the time and it gave me gas money and loafing money for Saturday night. Finally I did get a job with the company my Dad worked or. It was hard work, but the money was good for the time period. I guess you could say it was my first taste of the real world. I was starting to see why my Mother didn't want us to go out of the holler when we were young teenagers, or old teenagers, as far as that goes. Mom was real strict with all of us kids.

She was a no nonsense type, Dad wasn't near as bad but the first three of us kids were held to a real tight reign and I am sure that's why I did some of the crazy stuff I did when I was old enough to get out.

After I started working a steady job I decided to see if I couldn't get myself a little better car, something I could drive to work and back every day without having a break down. I found and bought a real nice 63 Chevy Impala. It was awesome, without a doubt the nicest car I had ever owned. I was in car heaven as far as I was concerned. It had a small V-8 engine and a 3 speed standard transmission and ran great, and yes I did drag race a little on the street, and never lost a race in that car. I am in no way condoning street racing but, what a rush!

One cold winter night I was out with one of my buddies just cruising and hanging out. I had to work the next day so we were not out too late. I dropped him off at the end of the road where he lived. I had just put new exhaust on my car and did not want to drag it in and out of the old muddy road he lived on. To this day that is all I remember of that night. My friend said he heard me pull out on the black top road that ran parallel to his road. He said he heard me go through the gears and then a loud crash. All I know is I wrecked on Tuesday night and did not come to my senses until Friday. My buddy told me later that I had been thrown through the windshield and landed in the creek. He ran across the bottom and got me out of the water before I drowned. Sounds reasonable to me, all I could do was take him at his word. Also the wreck happened right in front of a preacher's house. My friend told me later that the preacher came out to see if he could be of any assistance and he got down beside me in the creek and prayed for me. There is no doubt in my mind that is what saved my life on that cold November night. As I said before, I still do not remember the wreck at all, just very thankful to have survived. As for my little Chevy, it was killed that night. Nothing like being 18 and making car payments on a car that is in the junkyard. Needless to say I was off work for a while, I think about a month. I had received a very bad head injury and no matter your health and age, you can't just shake that off very easy. It was right around the first of the year when I went back to work. Life was good and about to get better. I did not know at the time, but in about three months we were going to move out of the holler, in fact out of the state. I was treated very well back on my job. I was allowed as much time to get back in the groove as I needed.

It was in the early spring of 1969 when Mom and Dad decided it was time to move out of the holler to bigger and better things I suppose. At least move a little closer to Dads work. They found a place just across the river in West Virginia to rent. So the decision was made for us to move. This was exciting and it really was a life altering experience for not only me, but the whole family. I remember loading up the old Chevy pickup truck with all the furniture and stuff we could get in it. Our road at that time was so wet and muddy the old truck was pretty much stuck as soon as I pulled out of the driveway. I had to walk out of the holler to a neighbor's house and ask him if he would bring his tractor and pull me out of the holler, he agreed and was glad to help. I had known this man all my life and worked for him on his farm. He was just a great man. As he pulled me through the mud and mess that was our road it was a bitter-sweet moment. We were actually moving out of the holler, I knew I would never forget the life and times of growing up there, and, I was right. I could not help but wonder what laid ahead for our family in another state.

As I look back on the hard times and growing up the way I did with my brother and sisters I can't help but think I would not want to do that again for any amount of money, however, I would not take any amount of money for my upbringing in the holler called Meadow Branch, Carter County, Rush, Kentucky.

I'm sure most people have heard the saying when someone was asked where they went to school and they would reply the School of Hard Knocks. That was about what life in the holler was like. As I reflect back on that lesson in life I have found, much to my surprise at times that education I got while growing up in the holler was indeed priceless. That was where you learned about life, all aspects. Manners, respect, self esteem and morals. Sometimes back then, yes, times were tough but the education for the body mind and soul was something great. You could not get it all out of a book, you had to live it.

I promise you though if you were living like we did it would be hard to explain to people at the time just how good an education in life they were getting. As I look back it certainly seems like that was another life time ago. I guess really that it was.

AUTHORS NOTE

As I look back at the 1950's and early 60's I realize now that what seemed like a depression to me, truly was a blessing in disguise. I honestly believe that if today's children had a little taste of the past we would all be better off in many, many ways. I thank God that I was born and raised in Eastern Kentucky and I will be an old head-of-the-holler Kentuckian until the day I die.

James A. Adkins

ABOUT THE AUTHOR

James Adkins and his wife Pamela live in southern Ohio near the banks of the Ohio River which borders eastern Kentucky, approximately 25 miles from where this story takes place. James is a retired truck driver, although he worked in various fields before settling into trucking. He has traveled the United States and Canada along with various countries worldwide. Never straying far from his childhood home as far as a permanent residence. James has entertained the thought of writing a book about his childhood for many years.

Jamesa1@zoominternet.net

Research tools: Google

Google Earth/Maps

Eastern Kentucky Maps

Kentucky Board of Education

CPSIA information can be obtained
at www.ICGtesting.com
Printed in the USA
LVHW090138040220
645691LV00004B/782